Introduction

Dinosaurs first roamed
the earth 245 million
years ago. Their bones,
dung, and tracks
have been found on
every **continent**.
Paleontologists are
still uncovering new
species of these **extinct**
prehistoric creatures
buried in sand, dried
mud, or rocks.
Get ready to meet the
most amazing dinosaurs!

Ankylosaurus

Ankylosaurus (AIN-kel-oh-soar-us) had armored eyelids. In fact, armor like a crocodile's thick skin covered its entire body to protect it from predators. It also protected itself by using the club at the end of the tail as a weapon. This North American dinosaur chomped on ferns with its leaf-shaped teeth and had a large stomach for digesting all those plants.

A full-grown *ankylosaurus* weighed the same as a baby blue whale.

Antarctopelta

Did you know that dinosaur bones have even been found in Antarctica? Digging up bones in the frosty continent is tricky because the ground is often frozen solid. *Antarctopelta* (ant-ark-toe-PELL-tah) was the first dinosaur found there in 1986. Believed to have been a plant eater, *Antarctopelta* was covered in armor to protect it from **predators**.

It took 10 years to dig up the rare **specimen** because of high winds and below-freezing temperatures.

Argentinosaurus

A turtle would tie in a race with slow-moving Argentinosaurus.

Argentinosaurus (ar-jen-tin-oh-SOAR-us) was one of the largest plant-eating land animals. A newborn *argentinosaurus* was only the size of a small dog, yet paleontologists estimate the giant weighed 75 tons (68.04 t) when full grown. That's the combined weight of about 150 polar bears! This South American dinosaur is known for fast growth. It could gain nearly 100 lbs. (45.36 kg) a day!

Brachiosaurus

Brachiosaurus (BRACK-ee-oh-soar-us) was a long-necked dinosaur. Its bones have been found in Africa, Europe, and North America. It used its towering neck, measuring five times the length of a giraffe's neck, to reach leaves from high branches. This **herbivore** ate as much as 900 lbs. (408.23 kg) of plants every day! That's the same as 11,000 cups (2602.47 L) of chopped broccoli.

Some scientists believe *brachiosauruses* weighed as much as 62 tons (56 metric tons), or as much as about 20 pickup trucks.

Brachylophosaurus'
skin would have
been as soft as
your earlobes.

Brachylophosaurus

Scientists in North America found a mummified duck-billed brachylophosaurus (brack-ill-off-oh-SOAR-us) they named Leonardo. A high-tech x-ray revealed stomach contents – chewed-up flowers, ferns, and even algae. The food preserved inside the stomach is a clue to this dinosaur's **habitat**. A portion of the body remains untouched for future paleontologists.

A *coelophysis* skull traveled to space on the Space Shuttle Endeavor as a link between the past and the future.

Coelophysis

Coelophysis (chell-AH-fis-iss) hatched from eggs. Dinosaur **embryos** developed for three to six months before they cracked through their shells. *Coelophysis* were 10 ft. (3.05 m) long and weighed between 33 and 44 lbs. (15 and 20 kg). These swift North American hunters could easily catch and feast on insects and small reptiles.

Microraptor

Dinosaurs could also be tiny. *Microraptor* (my-crow-RAPT-or) was slightly smaller than a parrot and, like wild parrots, lived among trees in the forest. Complete fossils of this four-winged dinosaur have been found in Asia. Prints of bone fragments in its stomach reveal *microraptor* feasted on small birds, reptiles, and even fish.

By making a life-sized model of *microraptor*, scientists found it could glide in the air but not flap its wings.

15

Nodosaur

In 2001, a man digging in a Canadian mine hit something very hard. What he found was a new type of fossilized *nodosaur* (NOD-oh-soar)—complete from the end of the snout to the hips. Scientists will soon give the dinosaur an official name. Researchers believe the herbivore never **decomposed** because it sank quickly to the bottom of sea and was immediately covered in **sediment**. The armor-covered fossil looks like a statue.

Scientists spent more than 7,000 hours scraping away the dirt that covered this newly found *nodosaur.*

Rhoetosaurus tracks reveal this dinosaur traveled in **herds**.

Rhoetosaurus

Rhoetosaurus (REET-oh-soar-us) was the first big dinosaur found in Australia. In the early 1920s, scientists found pieces of vertebrae, rib, leg, and tail bones. Fifty years later, paleontologists unearthed other pieces of leg and foot bones but still haven't found its skull and front legs. This creature was a *sauropod*, a large, long-necked, plant-eating machine that stood on all four feet.

Spinosaurus is named for its sail-shaped spine.

Spinosaurus

Spinosaurus (spine-oh-SOAR-us) was the largest **omnivore** ever to walk on land. The huge dinosaur walked on two hind legs and had two smaller front legs. But *Spinosaurus* also liked to swim and eat fish. **Fossils** found in Africa show that this dinosaur was at least 50 ft. (15.24 m) long—the length of five rhinos.

Stegosaurus

Stegosaurus (steg-oh-SOAR-us) had a zigzag row of pointy **dermal** plates along its back, making it look even longer than its bus-sized body. Its spiked tail helped scare away predators— an important trait for the slow-moving animal. This plant-eating, beaked dinosaur had only a few teeth in the back of its mouth and a brain the size of a hot dog. Paleontologists have found *stegosaurus* bones on four continents: Africa, Asia, Europe, and North America.

Stegosaurus swallowed stones to help mash up tough plants inside its stomach.

Triceratops

Triceratops (try-SARE-ah-tops) was a three-horned giant with a mouth full of 800 teeth. All those teeth were needed for this North American dinosaur to chew tough plants properly. Much has been learned about it since the late 1800s, when its huge skull was mistaken for a buffalo's. **Research** into the preserved stone footprints show *triceratops* ran faster than *Tyrannosaurus rex*.

Its three horns and frilled neck make triceratops one of the easiest dinosaurs to identify.

Tyrannosaurus rex

Scientists can learn what the dinosaur ate by studying its fossilized dung using a microscope.

Tyrannosaurus rex (tie-ran-oh-SOAR-us rex) is known as the tyrant lizard. With a mouth full of 60 pointed, banana-sized teeth, a *T. rex* could eat up to 500 lbs. (226.8 kg) of meat in one bite. That's like eating 2,000 hamburgers in one gulp! Front-facing eyes as big as baseballs helped this giant easily spot **prey**—including other *Tyrannosaurs*. Bones found in North America show this dinosaur would have been as long as a school bus!

Velociraptor

The turkey-sized *Velociraptor* (vel-ah-sih-RAPT-or) once lived in Asia. Despite its feathered body, the short-armed dinosaur had no wings and could not fly. Instead, the small but scary dinosaur chased prey by sprinting on two back legs and could run up to 50 mph (80.47 km)—as fast as a lion. The teeth curved backward, which made it difficult for its prey to escape a bite.

Velociraptor's feet each had a retractable claw that was about the length of a grizzly bear claw.

Glossary

continent
one of Earth's largest land masses that include Asia, Africa, North America, South America, Antarctica, Europe, and Australia

decomposed
decayed

dermal
of the skin

embryo
the early stage of development before birth or hatching

extinct
when a species no longer exists

fossil
a preserved imprint or remains of a plant or animal

habitat
a place where a living thing makes its home in nature

herbivore
a plant-eater

herd
animals that live, eat and travel together

omnivore
a meat-eater

paleontologist
a scientist who studies the remains of plants and animals

predator
an animal that hunts and eats other animals to survive

prehistoric
the time before history was recorded

prey
an animal that is hunted by other animals for food

sediment
what results when living and non-living material settle at the bottom of liquid

research
serious study to gather information on a subject

species
a group of similar living things

specimen
a collected sample

Written by Heather Villa

Illustrated by Simon Mendez

Designed by Bill Henderson

No part of this publication may be reproduced,
stored in a retrieval system, or transmitted in any form or by any means—
electronic, mechanical, photocopying, recording, or otherwise—
without written permission of Tangerine Press. All rights reserved.

an imprint of

www.scholastic.com

Published by Tangerine Press, an imprint of Scholastic Inc.
557 Broadway, New York, NY 10012

10 9 8 7 6 5 4 3 2 1

ISBN: 978-1-338-25739-7

Printed in Jiaxing, China

Photos ©: cover background: Joe Belanger/Shutterstock; inside front cover background: Authentic travel/
Shutterstock; back cover background and throughout: Toniflap/Shutterstock; 1 background: Toniflap/
Shutterstock; 2-3 background: Przemyslaw Wasilewski/Shutterstock; 3 bottom right: emka74/Shutterstock;
3 inset: Michael Smith ITWP/Shutterstock; 4-5 background: marktucan/Shutterstock; 4 bottom left: emka74/
Shutterstock; 4 inset: Moolkum/Shutterstock; 6-7 background: Marc Venema/Shutterstock; 6 bottom left:
kosmos111/Shutterstock; 6 inset: Volodymyr Burdiak/Shutterstock; 8-9 background: Toniflap/Shutterstock;
8 bottom left: Pavel Vakhrushev/Shutterstock; 10-11 background: Alexander Mazurkevich/Shutterstock;
10 bottom left: Pavel Vakhrushev/Shutterstock; 10 inset: Savelov Maksim/Shutterstock; 12-13 background:
Toma Bonciu/Dreamstime; 12 top left: Elenarts/Shutterstock; 12 inset: 3Dsculptor/Shutterstock; 15 bottom
right: Pavel Vakhrushev/Shutterstock; 16-17 background: www.sandatlas.org/Shutterstock; 17 bottom right:
Pavel Vakhrushev/Shutterstock; 17 inset: Robert Clark/National Geographic Creative; 18-19 background:
Bill45/Shutterstock; 18 bottom left: emka74/Shutterstock; 18 inset: jultud/Shutterstock; 20-21 background:
lazyllama/Shutterstock; 20 top left: kosmos111/Shutterstock; 22-23 background: Authentic travel/
Shutterstock; 23 top right: Pavel Vakhrushev/Shutterstock; 24-25 background: meistero/Shutterstock;
25 bottom right: emka74/Shutterstock; 26-27 background: Joe Belanger/Shutterstock; 26 bottom left: Pavel
Vakhrushev/Shutterstock; 29 top right: Elenarts/Shutterstock; 29 inset: W. Scott McGill/Shutterstock;
30-31 background: Toma Bonciu/Dreamstime; 32 background: Bill45/Shutterstock.